John Hogben

Richard Holt Hutton of the Spectator;

A monograph

John Hogben

Richard Holt Hutton of the Spectator;
A monograph

ISBN/EAN: 9783337731946

Printed in Europe, USA, Canada, Australia, Japan

Cover: Foto ©ninafisch / pixelio.de

More available books at **www.hansebooks.com**

RICHARD HOLT HUTTON

OF

'𝕿𝖍𝖊 𝕾𝖕𝖊𝖈𝖙𝖆𝖙𝖔𝖗'

A MONOGRAPH

EDINBURGH

OLIVER AND BOYD

LONDON: SIMPKIN, MARSHALL, HAMILTON, KENT AND CO.

1899

RICHARD HOLT HUTTON,

Born 2nd June 1826 ; *Died 9th September* 1897.

'Buried at Twickenham Parish Cemetery on
Tuesday, 15th September 1897. Round his
grave were grouped Anglicans, Roman
Catholics, Unitarians, in about equal numbers,
and in equal grief.'

The Academy, 18th September 1897.

CONTENTS

CHAP.   PAGE

  I. PERSONAL 9

 II. AS JOURNALIST . . . 35

III. AS CRITIC 49

IV. RELIGION 95

CHAPTER I

PERSONAL

'I WILL go forth 'mong men, not mailed in scorn,
But in the armour of a pure intent.
Great duties are before me .   .   .
.   .   .   .   .   when I fall
It matters not, so that God's work is done.
I've learned to prize the quiet lightning-deed,
Not the applauding thunder at its heels
Which men call Fame.'

ALEXANDER SMITH.

CHAPTER I

IT is certain that up till the day of his death Richard Holt Hutton was the most highly honoured of English journalists. His position indeed was in some ways unique, and it is worth remembering in these days that it was a position gained by the sheer uplifting power of supreme intellect and character. He belonged to no coterie. The log-roller passed him by on the other side. As for self-advertisement, everybody knows he loathed it. Although he stood so high, never was his power abused. He was, of course, far removed from the feeble folk who regard mere position as a valid excuse for the sin of emptiness. To these, indeed, he belonged not at all ; yet he might sometimes have been tempted to speak in the accents of the

conqueror. He never did so. Not for that
reason has his truer promotion tarried.

In having left an expressed desire that no
formal memoir of themselves should be written,
Mr Hutton and Dean Church entail a real loss
on many earnest and thoughtful people, who, it
may well be, abhor the fashionable multiplication
of trivial incidents about vain and flippant
writers that have merely amused the public for
a few years, but who would, on the other hand,
richly esteem a record of the larger outlines of
a noble life, and lay to heart the wisdom and the
healing strength that might be gathered from
letters which passed between friend and friend.
'Next to a man's own work,' wrote Dr Marcus
Dods recently in reviewing the life of a promi-
nent Englishman, 'a good biography is his best
memorial.' The loss is ours, and no adequate
compensation is found in the added admiration
with which we find men who have held a com-
manding position in the world, refraining from
seeking popular applause in a day when the
interviewer is king — the more impudent, the
more thought of in many quarters—and the
flattering paragraph, inspired often by the
flattered writer himself, is ubiquitous.

Mr Hutton himself, it may be remembered, in

his memoir of William Caldwell Roscoe, his
brother-in-law, quotes with approval a passage
from a review by that fascinating writer, dealing
with this very question of the written lives of
men. The particular reference has to do with
men whose actions and achievements in the
open daylight of the world form their own
best monument, and who, therefore, least need
biography. Roscoe writes, 'When, however,
personal character is the main source of their
influence on others,—when the unconscious
labourer, pressing forward in faithful service,
reflects a glory from his upturned counten-
ance, scatters the fire of his aspiration in sur-
rounding hearts, and by subtle impress of
spirit upon spirit, refines conscience, warms
enthusiasm, and quickens effort — then it
is that a life, a record, a *portrait* is most
needed. The chief work, indeed, is done
without it ; many a heart moulded, many a
course changed, many a soul set in motion, puri-
fied, redeemed by contact with the living man ;
and the influence spreads from mind to mind
like circles in the water. But like such circles,
this influence grows less discernible and fainter
as it spreads, and it is a great thing to stamp with
permanence its original sources, however inade-

quate and fragmentary may be the image pre-
served.' Having quoted these words, Mr Hutton
remarks that this view applies peculiarly to a
man of Roscoe's stamp, and he uses the passage,
one cannot but feel, as a salve for his conscience
in departing from his own inbred delight in
silence on such matters. It is plainly felt by him
to be *his* justification for writing a memoir of
Roscoe, and many, thinking the words closely
concern such a life as Mr Hutton's own, will in
their turn feel disposed to find in them a warrant
for saying something of such a man as the
editor of the *Spectator* himself. His life was
certainly not one of action in the sense that the
soldier's or the sailor's is ; but it was none the
less one that covered much ground ; for the
mind travels as does the body, only with in-
finitely more wonderful means of motion at
command. Nor is the country traversed by the
mind smaller in dimensions. It taketh up the
isles as a very little thing. Is it of no interest
to trace the growth of a mind? Wordsworth
answered the question—more wisely than many
who sneer at him think—in over 8000 lines ;
and Mr Hutton's own feeling is, that the finer
the qualities discerned in the outgrowths and
efforts of any mind, the more do we wish to know

of it. It is easy to lapse into a know-nothing state, and remain there. Probably, however, interest in the history of the mind that so settles down, ends with the *beginning* of its more or less stationary Agnosticism. It is otherwise when a man has 'wrestled on towards Heaven,' or Truth, or Right, or Beauty, or whatever one may choose to call it, and come upon something to rest in—above all, something buoyant and sustaining, leaving well-defined footprints as he goes his way. To have such a chart, with something of its true literary and ethical settings, is certainly to add life to life. Surely sooner or later a book about Richard Holt Hutton answering to this description will see the light.

It was inevitable that there should be various readings of Mr Meredith Townsend's *Spectator* paragraph as to Mr Hutton. For the most part a respectful silence followed the announcement of the death. It is true almost every journal of note paid its tribute, but the notices were restrained and formal, and very little of a biographical nature crept out. They formed, as the *Westminster Gazette* expressed it, 'the record of a splendid mind rather than the story of the life of a man.' Yet Mr Townsend can never have thought for a moment that what is more

or less public property already, would fail to
come forth some time or other; although he, of
all men, *the* one who could have told us most—
holds his peace. As for Mr Hutton himself,
never in the most modest mood of a most
modest man's life, can it have been quite possible
for him to imagine that his great services to
journalism, to literature, to thought, and to
theology, should be rewarded by a chill silence ;
and it seems to the writer not only possible
but necessary to read in his expressed wish that
no biography of himself should be written, no
harsh voice compelling men to think of him
only as a light that failed when Death blew.
He eagerly sought to declare himself when he
was with us, and his words at least remain. It
can be no sin against dead or living to recall
the written words. It must be remembered
that in all probability Mr Hutton had more
than personal reasons in forbidding a biography,
and it may be taken for granted that such a
biography as he feared will never be published.
Meantime these pages profess to give nothing
but a mere outline of a great man's written
work, and although the present writer has ready
to hand many details of the outer life of Mr
Hutton, he prefers studiously to avoid every-

thing that might make of his brochure anything of the nature of a memoir.   After all, the
particulars of the life are simple, and all, we may
be sure, free from taint.   There is no buzz of
society's flies over this man ; no mystery, the
solution of which hangs heavy on the shallow-
minded.

How the subject of this monograph prepared
himself for his work on the great English newspaper he was to control, may be gathered from
the following story for which Mr T. H. S.
Escott is responsible :—'The Roman historian,
Mommsen, now Professor at Berlin, delivered in
Hutton's time some lectures at Bonn.   The first
question the Teuton *savant* put to an English
visitor in the year 1883, related to the British
student who had attended his classes, and who
had since become known throughout Europe,
alike by his newspaper and his independent
writings.   "That young man," were Mommsen's
words, "took away from my lectures not only all
the knowledge I could give him, but much
mental nutriment, for which he was indebted to
his own genius."'   The same authority (Mr
Escott), writing in days when Mr Hutton was
amongst us and busy at his work, states that his
student days in Rhineland 'were turned to such

B

account as to equip him with a rare knowledge
of modern literature in all countries and in all
languages of Europe. The habit of omnivorous
reading has never forsaken him, so that the
Spectator's joint editor stands forth to-day among
publicists as a prodigy of diversified culture.'
This being so, was there ever a man who made
less parade of his knowledge and accomplishments ? In his early years, the Unitarian paper
known as the *Inquirer* afforded him an excellent
opportunity of working his way towards his
true vocation. If not actually editor, he took a
leading part in that journal's production, and as
evidence of a growing disinclination to pulpit
work, he has himself set on record that even
then his mind was turning from mere preaching
towards the fuller form of worship the Church of
England supplies, for this is surely the meaning
of such words as these : 'I attempted to prove
that the laity ought to have the protection
offered by a liturgy against the arbitrary prayers
of the minister, and next that, at least, the
great majority of the sermons ought to be suppressed, and the habit of delivering them dis-
continued altogether.' These are, I think
strictly present-day views in many quarters.
So fierce were the articles written by what

was called a knot of young Unitarians, that Mr Hutton long afterwards wrote in semi-pitiful words, which had withal a touch of pride in the long-abandoned religious community wherein he had been reared :—'Only a denomination of just men made all but "perfect" would have tolerated it at all.' All this happened as long ago as 1851. It is not to be denied that the phrase 'A Stickit Minister,' as applied to Mr Hutton, made an admirable catch-penny head-line. But it is one that jars. As well might Canon Ainger's books on Lamb bear for their title, 'An East India House Clerk.' Nevertheless it is quite true that he failed to find the pulpit he sought for at one time ; in which, had he found it, he would probably not have remained long. I do not think Unitarianism could have held him any more than it could hold Coleridge. It is said that Frederick Denison Maurice remarked to Mr Solly that the best article on his theological essays had appeared in the *Prospective Review*, and that he should like to know the author. The writer was R. H. Hutton, and the two, as we know, became fast friends for life. In time the Unitarian standpoint was abandoned, and Mr Hutton became a very pronounced Churchman, who, while not exactly fitting into any of the great sections in the State Church, had some of the best qualities of each of what are known as Broad, High, and Low ; although, it must be added, he very much disliked the last as a party. Latterly he was generally designated a High Churchman. By-and-bye he became editor of the *National Review* (not, of course, the present monthly of that name), a Quarterly of solidity and strength, which, however, never succeeded, although it was ably governed by Mr Hutton, and financed, it is said, by Lady Byron. The mention of the existing *National Review*, of which the present poet-laureate was for some time joint editor with Mr Courthope, reminds one that an ill-mannered but feeble attack on Mr Hutton, *apropos* of his warmly expressed admiration for Clough, appeared in Mr Alfred Austin's book 'The Poetry of the Period,' published in 1870. The two men afterwards, however, became quite friendly, and Mr Austin's verse sometimes found its way into the *Spectator*. Although the earlier *National Review* was not a financial triumph, Dr Robertson Nicoll, who professes to have read almost every word of it, gives it as his opinion, that 'no such excellent review has ever been published in England.'

It was a happy destiny that brought Meredith Townsend and Richard Holt Hutton together. Mr Townsend had returned from India, having given up the *Friend of India*, and had purchased the *Spectator*, then on the down-grade— Mr Hutton being at that time about thirty-five years of age—with the result that the two men have furnished, as one of them has said, the spectacle of 'an unbroken friendship of thirty-six years, and a literary alliance, which at once in its duration and completeness is probably without a precedent.' The rest of his literary career, as editor of the Wellington Street organ, we know.

In spite of the paucity of biographical details, it is pleasant to find here and there, in out-of-the-way places sometimes, detached but interesting incidents in Mr Hutton's life, related by himself in moments of vivid retrospection ; and following the lines indicated at the beginning of this booklet, I shall not go beyond his own self-disclosures. It is noteworthy that it is when he is writing of other men's doings and sayings—perhaps only then— that he drops hints, and flashes side-lights on his own career and history. There is one book, it is true, in which he speaks out a little more plainly and at greater length than elsewhere, namely in 'Holiday Rambles in Ordinary Places by a Wife with her Husband.' The contents of the book are in the form of letters addressed to the editor of the *Spectator*. In the advertisement they are called slight narratives of holiday travel, and something like an apology is given for their reproduction. No such thing is needed. They are singularly fresh and racy, especially the lady's contributions. These latter are, indeed, what Mrs Carlyle, had she been another man's wife, might have written, but they belong, on the whole, to a sweeter, if less intense nature than Mrs Carlyle's, even as that nature might have been when it belonged to plain Jane Welsh. The letters have no bite in them ; or, if this is going too far, one may say it is only the lip-bite of love, as, for example, when the lady ventures to say of her husband in his own newspaper such a thing as this : ' He has a lot of cobwebs somewhere at the bottom of his dear addled old brain.'

These letters consist of six series, and are pleasantly humorous, being filled with en-

thusiastic appreciation of Arnold's and Wordsworth's poetry. There are everywhere present
indications of the genuinely warm yet playful
relationship which existed between husband
and wife. They are doubly interesting as
affording us a picture of Mr Hutton on holiday.
He is said to have liked driving, but he had
few other outdoor pastimes of the more active
kind. Maurice once wrote to Kingsley about
the enjoyment many men have in games and
sport. There is something pathetic but very
characteristic in the manner in which he stated
that he had ' tried to feel no grudge against those
who have that which my conscience tells me it
is not a virtue but a sin to want.' There is
nothing of this apologetic spirit in Mr Hutton,
although there is not a little of the same restriction of his open-air enjoyments. He had small
interest in the glorification of the killing instinct
which is dignified by the name of sport, and he
once reflected with evident relish, in a letter to
the present writer, that the ' golfers in England
were still in a hopeless minority.' In the
Ammergau letters, there are some references
to the state of Paris at the time. Mrs Hutton
writes in a mock-fearful manner in one of these
dated from Berne, 12th August 1870 :—' An

Englishman shot by order of the Government as a Prussian spy! Imagine my consternation. Why, Edward [who stands, of course, for her husband] is precisely the sort of person to get shot as a Prussian spy. I don't mean that he looks like a spy, but he has a large beard and is horribly short-sighted, and looks like a book-worm, and has German books in his bag, and he, unfortunately, has a habit—got from our many weeks' travel in Germany—of saying " herein " instead of " come in," when anybody knocks at the door, a habit by which a German waiter in a French inn has more than once found out that German is the right language to talk to him in ; and then he is very imprudent in his talk, and is just as certain to revile the Emperor in France as in Switzerland.' Another letter from Berne gives a description of a sunset seen from the cathedral terrace. Mrs Hutton breaks out in a complaining way, through the transparency of which one sees the pride she had in her husband :—' Edward, whose mind was in the scene before Sedan, and who can talk of nothing but what he calls the moral causes for the Prussian victories and for the ruin of the French empire, was muttering audibly enough, " I know that all things come to an end, but Thy commandment is exceeding broad."' In yet another letter of about the same date, the lady writes :—' It is a pity my dear, good Edward is so short-sighted and so invincibly ignorant of flowers. He delights in them, and has got quite a passion for finding me new ones—but then his blindness ! Only think, on the Pass of Oberalp, above Andermatt, he was picking me a fine potato-flower, such as Frank had his first lesson on in Miss Edgeworth's story, as something new and fascinating. I asked him if we should dry it and take it home, labelled, " *Solanum tuberosum Alpinum ;* habitat, ploughed fields and rifts of the lower Alps." Was not that delicious ? However, when I was on a mule, he really got me a good many pretty flowers, when they were carefully pointed out to him.' All through the letters there are delightful feminine freaks, and Mr Hutton's contributions are evidently written up, so to speak, as far as his heavier tones will allow, to his wife's soprano. It has been said that the one accessible glimpse of his private life is to be found in this book of travellers' letters. This is not strictly the case, however, for in the memoir prefixed to ' The Literary Studies of Walter Bagehot,' whom elsewhere he describes as his

most intimate friend, we get glimpses of another
sort. 'I first met Bagehot,' writes he, 'at
University College, London, when we were
neither of us over seventeen. Once, I remember, in the vehemence of our argument
as to whether the so-called logical principle of
identity (A is A) were entitled to rank as a law
of thought, or only as a postulate of language,
Bagehot and I wandered up and down Regent
Street for something like two hours in the vain
attempt to find Oxford Street.' The account of
the Metaphysical Society which he has given us in
a *Nineteenth Century* article may be fitly brought
into line with this picture of the two young
men walking about Regent Street. It is perfectly evident in Mr Hutton's books, and in
many a *Spectator* article, how keenly he
turned to the consideration of a subtle subject.
The paper referred to is one of an extraordinary kind. Perhaps no other member of the
society—and it is not too much to say that
every member was a man of note—could have
written it. It describes a supposed debate
in the society, the various speakers being
sketched with wonderful exactness. While
the words are Mr Hutton's, the views are
those of each of the men represented. The

whole is worked out with admirable freedom and effect. 'The article,' writes Mr Knowles, the editor of the *Nineteenth Century*, 'is not a portrait of any actual meeting, but a reminiscence of the sort of debate which used to go on. Its faithfulness is remarkable, except for the omission of his own valuable part in the discussion,' all mention of which is, of course, characteristically avoided. This compliment was emphasised and enlarged upon by Professor Huxley; and Dean Church used to tell how a fillip was often given to the discussion, by Mr Hutton rising, when interest flagged, and carrying the subject along newer and deeper channels. To read this article is to see the editor of the *Spectator* in his element. We feel that the members of the society are actually moving before us. One comes under the spell of what is called 'the wistful and sanguine . . . hectic idealism of James Hinton'; 'the noble and steadfast, but somewhat melancholy faith, which seemed to be sculptured on Dr Martineau's massive brow, shaded off into wistfulness in the glance of the eyes.' Here are the alert Professor Huxley, whose 'slender definite creed' in no respect, Mr Hutton thought, 'represented the cravings of his large nature'; the ascetic

Archbishop — afterwards Cardinal — Manning,
every nerve in whose face was 'expressive of
some vivid feeling'; and Mr Ruskin with his
'deep-toned musical voice.' It is not the
extraordinary grasp of a subtle subject from
any one point of view that is noteworthy; it is
the great imaginative sympathy that is revealed
here, and, indeed, in a great many of Mr
Hutton's best essays. In this paper, one may
say in passing, we are reminded of another not-
able feature in his writings, and that is his vivid
power of portraiture, by means of which, in a
few sentences, he depicts the deeper man that
lies behind the familiar features that face the
outer world. Take only one example. 'Most
of us know by bust, photograph, or picture, the
wonderful face of the great Cardinal [Newman,
of course], that wide forehead, ploughed deep
with parallel horizontal furrows, which seem to
express his careworn grasp of the double aspect
of human nature, its aspect in the intellectual,
and its aspect in the spiritual world, the pale
cheek down which—

> " Long lines of shadows slope,
> Which years, and curious thought and suffering give,"

the pathetic eye which speaks compassion from

afar, and yet gazes wonderingly into the impass-
able gulf which separates man from man, and the
strange mixture of asceticism and tenderness in all
the lines of that mobile and reticent mouth where
humour, playfulness and sympathy are intricately
blended with those severer moods that "refuse
and restrain." On the whole, it is a face full, in
the first place, of spiritual passion of the highest
order, and in the next, of that subtle and intimate knowledge of the details of human limita-
tion and weakness which makes all spiritual
passion look utterly ambitious and hopeless,
unless indeed, it be guided amongst the stakes
and dykes and pitfalls of the human battlefield
by the direct providence of God.' This seems
to me a delineation worthy of being placed
beside Carlyle's interpretation of Dante's face.
I must confess the temptation is strong to re-
produce also the picture of Maurice as he appeared to Hutton, when Bagehot — then a
student of Lincoln's Inn—took him to hear one
of the afternoon sermons by the chaplain of
the Inn. Reverting for a moment to the two
volumes of W. C. Roscoe's essays and poems,
which were edited by Mr Hutton, we get some
other personal traits. 'I vividly remember,'
writes he, 'the embarrassment with which when

he [Roscoe] occupied the chair in the College Debating Society, I used to catch his eye gravely fixed on me as I uttered my boyish eloquence or my fanatical political creed. The carefully prepared metaphor, or the abstract principles of political justice which were there poured forth, often came to a premature close under the expression of fixed attention and consideration with which he surveyed the speakers.' Through Roscoe, probably, was engendered that love of the lower animals so characteristic of the editor of the *Spectator*. It may be remembered by readers of 'Holiday Rambles' that on returning home the husband and wife heard the doleful tale of their strayed Persian cat, but found three tails wagging vigorously as ever as their possessors rushed to meet the wanderers,—which goes to prove that Mr Hutton's interest in animals was not merely a curious study confined to the busy hours he spent at Wellington Street, but took practical shape in flesh and blood at home. To return to Roscoe. 'I remember,' writes Hutton, 'I was exposed on more than one occasion to his good - humoured raillery for my shameless ignorance of such matters. He had a standing joke against me on the blankness of mind which I once betrayed as to

the nature of the nylghau ; and he scoffed at
me much for some blind assertion which I made,
as I believed on authority, that the " conies " in
the 104th Psalm were a sort of rabbit.' It was
Roscoe, by the way, who wrote to Hutton in
light vein when the latter seemed bound up in
graver subjects : 'You are becoming absolutely Scotch : Your way of regarding any
approach to a mild joke or any departure from
the directest simplicity of statement. It is
very sad to see a man endowed by nature with
a considerable appreciation of humour, losing it,
like a stream swallowed up in the sands of
political economy. I presume you now talk
" Bank " at dinner, and that your reins in the
night season summon you to meditate on the
" history of prices." Hasten therefore into
Wales. Here we talk of pigs. We ask ourselves whether bean-meal will pay for cows to
eat, and solve moral questions as to mixing old
and new milk. Puns are still made in these
rural districts, and we lead an existence independent of figures. We cannot understand the
return of the Bank of England accounts, and
though very glad to know " how they would
show under the old system " have not the least
idea how to do the sum.'

These little sketches of the man as he appeared at various times in his life, and under different conditions, have been dwelt on thus long, for they are after all autobiographical outlines. Broken indeed are the lines, but they suggest how the unfinished picture may be filled out in its larger significance. A finished portrait of himself he has certainly not supplied. It was not, indeed, without a grim smile that one looked in vain for a black and white portrait in the illustrated papers which commented on Mr Hutton's death. In an age which rains photographs, wherein cameras are as common as paving-stones and as relentless as road-engines, here was one man at least who had apparently escaped them all, whose portrait seemed as scarce as Miss Marie Corelli's own—nay, more so, for has not that lady at last suffered from a snap-shot, the result of which may be seen, in the *Lady's Realm*? But although Mr Hutton's photograph was not forthcoming in the public prints, the original was in the habit of making public appearances at the Church Congress and elsewhere, so that he was not altogether confined to his editor's room, and people now and again saw and heard him on various platforms. His last Church Congress paper was read—he did not

always read his own papers — at Folkestone in
1892. We have seen already how short-sighted
he was, and no one who has had the almost
painful pleasure of hearing him lecture, is likely
to forget the strongly-marked face, the almost
touching anxiety to make himself heard, while he
hid his face in his beard, and muffled the sound
of his voice in the MS., which he was obliged to
hold close to his eye—he had only *one* available—
the reading-lamp requiring to be specially adjusted until it almost touched his eyebrows.
Whether his weak vision was chargeable wholly—
it must have had some say in the matter—with
his penmanship or not, the fact remains that he
shared with Dean Stanley—whose caligraphy was
somewhat similar to his own in character—the
reputation of being probably the worst pen-
man among the literary men of England.

CHAPTER II

AS JOURNALIST

' THE Editor is bound to lend a patient hearing to the most paradoxical opinions and extravagant theories which have resulted in our times from the " infinite agitation of wit," but he is disposed to qualify them by a number of practical objections, of speculative doubts, of checks and drawbacks, arising out of actual circumstances and prevailing opinions, or the frailties of human nature. He has a great range of knowledge, an incessant activity of mind. . . . His pen is never at a loss, never stands still.'

WILLIAM HAZLITT.

CHAPTER II

OF the *Spectator* itself what shall be said? Mr Hutton's connection with the journal dated from 1861, and it is not too much to say that its position during his reign has been unequalled. Whether we believe the statement or not, the words give some idea of the reputed influence of the *Spectator*, when we find it soberly set down in a journal not given to exaggeration, that if Mr Hutton's paper 'had supported Home Rule, or had even observed a benevolent neutrality, it is probable that Mr Gladstone's Bill of 1886 would have passed the House of Commons. The *Spectator* did more than all the rest of the Anti-Home Rule London Press to consolidate the opposition to Mr Gladstone's Irish policy.' In an article in the *Bookman* written a year or two ago, it was stated that probably no English journal wielded a stronger influence over thoughtful men. It was, until the other day, owned by two men only, who were also its editors, and it is said that their contributions never averaged less than two articles each, besides occasional reviews, and most of the paragraphs in the summary of the week's news.   One who described herself as having listened for thirty years to Mr Hutton's voice, truly remarked about his newspaper, that we cut it open with as much confidence as we broke the seal dropped by a friendly hand.   The pages of the journal, its regular readers felt, did not surprise, did not even entertain so much as sustain.   It has been called ' above all journals a journal written by gentlemen for gentlemen.' One knows in these days how much such a phrase means.   It has been no society journal, gentlemanly or otherwise.   How the world moves, concerned it only as regards a form of motion that Shakspere's word ' wags ' does not aptly describe.   So much fairness is in it—one is most unwilling to use the past tense yet—that it is easily understood how a *Saturday* reviewer should come to confess, as one really did, that a difficulty in the way of his reading the paper lay in its being so just.   The review represented by this reviewer in noticing Mr Hutton's death, spoke, it may be remembered, of the public addressed by the *Spectator* as 'a public sheltered in leafy rectories and in snug villas of rich non-conformists from the headlong decisions and rowdy activity of the world.' It is truly in this total absence of rowdyism—one gives the word which includes plenty of genteel life so-called, a wide application,—and in this bringing in of salvation from headlong decisions that the *Spectator* excels. It has often been said that the times have changed, and that the day of the high-priced weekly has passed away never to return. One would fain hope the other way. It is true one can scarcely in these days characterise all newspapers in the language Crabbe employed : at the same time one meets every day of the week men who confess that many daily papers, with their eternal pother over squabbles, municipal, political, or ecclesiastical (which one might call tempests in tea-cups, were this not to libel an excellent beverage and an often artistically adorned vessel of honour), with their hopeless lack of any real sense of proportion, and their eternal foisting upon their readers that which points to their own gain, provoke and deserve nothing but contempt. Out of all this arises the impression, —which requires, no doubt, courage to carry forward into act,—that we should emphatically know more of what is worth knowing by reading a weekly paper which has in its editorial chambers a powerful winnowing mill and a rubbish shoot of wide dimensions ; which, in a leisurely way, waits until one lie disposes of another, and the truth at length falls on both ; wherein well-reasoned articles appear, and where reviews of books do not come upon us with such indecent haste as they do in some daily papers that sacrifice nearly everything to what is called smartness. One naturally recalls in this connection what Mr Gladstone said to a writer of one of the obituary notices of Mr Hutton :—'The *Spectator* is one of the few papers which are written in the fear and love of God,' and also what Maurice wrote of the press generally. In a letter to Sir T. Acland, he said :—' Have you meddled with periodicals, and have you thanked God that you still think, love, go to church, and find any one to love you ?' Of course, we all fortunately know of many noble exceptions, and there is no occasion just yet to give our pessimism the rein and say of these days, with the late laureate :—

' They are the new dark ages, you see, of the popular press.'

To return to the *Spectator:* One of the
best things one may say of it is, that it is a
paper that has known its way. As for its
summary of the week's events, more than
one man of note describes it, both as regards
its meritorious omissions and its concise presentment of the great events that transpire
week by week, as quite the best bit of
journalism in the English press. The whole
journal, indeed, with its fine wholesomeness,
its unusual fairness, its suppressed power, its
anything but supercilious corrective tone, has
about it a quieting effect compared with the
hot hurried developments of a press whose
note is mere cleverness, and what is known
as up-to-dateness. The up-to-date man may
be, and often is, the man for whom the
yesterdays which give to-day a great deal of its
beauty and force, have no charm. It has been
finely said by Mr William Wallace that 'Mr
Hutton's paper represents, at its richest, the
serious thought of the serious yet cultured
Englishman who likes to keep abreast of the
times, but is incapable of breaking abruptly or
irreverently with the past.' The *Spectator* has
always seemed, to one of its readers at least,
as nearly as possible an ideal paper for a

cultured, discriminating, leisurely life, which is,
however, not too self-indulgent to overlook the
more vital movements of the world, although
ready, delightedly enough, to 'avert its ken'
from more than half of the human fate on
which, as represented in print, multitudes
voraciously feed. To say that the periodical
is noted for its earnestness, is certainly not,
even in frivolous days like these, to say anything against it. Mrs Hutton wrote playfully
in one of the holiday letters which have been
already referred to, 'By the way, I should much
like to have the *Spectator's* view—the earnest
view, you know—of mothers-in-law.' In this
we have a true touch, as in many other things
spoken in jest, for there is nothing in existence
that might not be *earnestly* viewed in the
pages of the journal without our feeling it to
be out of place. After all, do we know of
any single periodical which comprises within
itself more of 'the things that are more excellent,' and fewer references to things we can
best spare in newspapers? Its literary findings
have neither been few nor unimportant. The
pronounced manner in which it has heralded
many great books, finds an apt illustration in
the words of Professor Henry Drummond: 'I

well remember,' writes he, 'when the first thunderbolt from the English critics penetrated my fastness. One night, an hour after midnight, my camp was suddenly roused by the apparition of three black messengers, dispatched from the north end of Lake Nyassa by a friendly white, with the hollow skin of a tiger-cat, containing a small package of letters and papers. Lighting the lamp in my tent I read the letters, and then turned over the newspapers, the first I had seen for many months. Among them was a copy of the *Spectator*, containing a review of "Natural Law," a review, with criticism enough in it, certainly, to make one serious, but written with that marvellous generosity and indulgence to an unknown author for which the *Spectator* stands supreme in journalism. I shall perhaps the less regret being betrayed into these personal reminiscences that I have the opportunity before I close of acknowledging a favour which I cannot forget. Why any critic should have risked his own reputation by speaking with such emphasis of the work of a new and un-practised hand, remains to me among the mysteries of literary unselfishness and charity. I am sure it was largely owing to this anonymous benefaction that when I returned to England I found the book had been given a hearing before many others which deserved it more.'

A well-known London editor once told the present writer that in his judgment no review printed elsewhere had anything like so powerful an effect on the sale of a book as one appearing in the *Spectator*. Mr Hutton's passionate appreciation of the poetry of Mr William Watson is still fresh in our memories. The author of 'Wordsworth's Grave' has not been niggardly in showing his gratitude. He has dedicated 'Lachrymæ Musarum' to the editors of the *Spectator* by name ; he has coupled Mr Hutton's name, individually, in an ardent stanza or two, with the names of Schubert and Shakspere, as chief factors in bringing happiness into his life ; and he has also written a paper on Mr Hutton in the *Bookman*, afterwards printed in his prose volume 'Excursions in Criticism.' Mr Watson confesses himself struck, like many others, with the solidarity of the *Spectator*. 'Mr Hutton,' writes he, '*is* the *Spectator*.' He quotes Professor Earle who calls the well-known weekly 'the most remarkable example of a journal, which, for any diversity of tone, or manner, or attitude, you can detect in its articles, might be written by one man from cover to cover.' Mr Watson is assuredly not shooting beyond the mark when he calls the *Spectator* 'the most entirely respected newspaper printed in the English language.' The sentence in which he speaks of Mr Hutton as a literary critic seems to me to show true discrimination. 'We feel,' writes he, 'that here is a mind of great opulence, which yet positively refuses to deploy its forces for the mere purpose of intellectual parade or display. It is perhaps almost too engrossed in the more serious object of capturing the coy and elusive truth, and not the truth which is minor and subsidiary, but the truth of most value and moment to the human soul.' How did Mr Hutton take all this? Such a book as 'Excursions in Criticism' was bound, on account of its intrinsic merits alone, to be favourably reviewed in the *Spectator*, and one cannot fail to see the pen of Mr Hutton in the review, and particularly in the expressed belief that the paper on himself should have been omitted from the volume. It is worth while quoting his words, not only to show the modesty of the reviewer—a fact well enough known already—but as affording a view of his impressions of his co-editor, Mr Townsend, who has been, one fears, overshadowed beyond his deserts by the greater personality of his colleague. The *Spectator* speaks of 'the genial article on one of the editors of this journal—very far from the more important of them'—and proceeds: 'The greater qualities of journalists are not literary, but political; and in the political field, large historical knowledge and high political imagination are far the most essential of the journalistic gifts, and are gifts to which the subject of Mr Watson's genial essay has no pretension.'

When Mr Morley brought out his edition of Wordsworth for Messrs Macmillan, it was, I think, Professor Dowden who described, with some cruelty and not a little truth, the laudatory essay prefixed to the volume, as of interest chiefly as an indication of the length the poet's voice carried, in reaching the future biographer of Gladstone. Mr Hutton's influence seems to have reached great distances and moved very diverse personalities. We have Mr Stead, for example, acknowledging that 'his was the ablest pen that was constantly employed in British journalism for the last thirty years,' and confessing, with evident sincerity, that while many would say he had less in common with the editor of the *Spectator* than with any other editor, he nevertheless, 'owed more as a journalist to Mr Hutton than to any other of his craft.' Another journalist, whose opinion has already been quoted in this appreciation, does not hesitate to state that Mr Hutton's writings give in spirit 'the high-water mark of self-respecting journalism,' and asserts that in respect of the impossibility of his thinking or writing on a low intellectual or moral plane, 'Mr Hutton is to the journalism of the last twenty-five years what Mr Gladstone has been to the politics of the same period.' . . . He also adds: 'I doubt whether any public writer of the present generation or its predecessor has on the spur of the moment said so many true and sagacious things with so much point.' It were easy to move from praise to praise. When a literary lady said to Dr Robertson Nicoll that the only two journalists of genius in the London press were Mr Townsend and Mr Hutton, the editor of the *British Weekly* tells us he could not see his way to disagree. Fairness to his opponents begot even in them a kind of loyalty to Mr Hutton, and as nothing is more characteristic of him than the desire to place himself close to those who understood him least, we may take leave of him as a journalist in words written six years ago in a paper which is politically an opponent of the *Spectator* : ' Bit by bit the conviction has been forced upon many of us that if English journalism has a chief—and even a Republic acknowledges a head—he is to be found in Mr Hutton. Whether with him or against him they [readers of his journal] have never lost the impression that they were in the presence of a strong individuality, a powerful mind and a noble soul—the very type of a fair and honourable journalist whom no man might fear to meet in open contest, and whose blows, however hard they might be, would never be aimed below the belt.'

CHAPTER III

AS CRITIC

D

'To be useful to as many as possible is the especial duty of a critic, and his utility can only be attained by rectitude and precision. He walks in a garden which is not his own; and he neither must gather the blossoms to embellish his discourse, nor break the branches to display his strength. Rather let him point to what is out of order, and help to raise what is lying on the ground.'

WALTER SAVAGE LANDOR.

CHAPTER III

MR HUTTON's main work was, of course, associated with the *Spectator*, and it may surely be added that his high personal character was in itself an influence that powerfully operated side by side with the labours of his pen. Busy journalist though he was, however, he has not left himself without a witness in book-land ; and it is consolatory to remember that although the great journalist is gone, the written book remains. Besides editing the Biographical, Literary, and Economic studies of W. Bagehot, and writing his memoir, and also editing, with a memoir, W. C. Roscoe's Poems and Essays, Mr Hutton has placed the thoughtful public under permanent obligation by publishing the following volumes : ' The Relative Value of Studies and Accomplishments in the Education of Women,'—a lecture (1862) ; 'Studies in Parliament,'—a series of sketches of leading politicians, reprinted from the *Pall Mall Gazette* (1866); 'Essays, Theological and Literary,'—in 2 vols. (1871); the delightful anonymous volume already alluded to, 'Holiday Rambles in Ordinary Places, by a Wife with her Husband,'—(1877); 'Essays on Modern Guides of English Thought in matters of Faith,'—(1887); 'Criticisms on Contemporary Thought and Thinkers,'—2 vols. (1894). He also contributed the 'Scott' volume to Mr Morley's 'English Men of Letters' series, and the 'Newman' volume to the 'English Leaders of Religion' series.

When the nature of the work is considered—even making due allowance for the portion of it which has been reprinted from the *Spectator*—this cannot but be regarded as a formidable output for a man actively engaged in more temporary business. The 'Studies in Parliament' attracted considerable attention, both in their original quarters in the *Pall Mall Gazette* and on their separate publication in book form by Longmans. Even at this date they afford excellent reading, although some of the studies concern themselves with politicians who have gone their way out of our lives and almost out of our memories. Nor will it be gainsayed that

in these portraits a quite uncommon power of
characterisation is displayed, mingled with
weighty verdict and shrewd outlook into the
future of those who were at that date young
men. The papers are in themselves short, but
they are abundantly pithy and full of good
things—full too of a directness and fearless
frankness that are refreshing even when we feel
compelled to differ from the writer. The preface
informs us that they are for the most part
opinions 'not hastily formed, but, of course,
formed without any advantages except those of
an outside, though interested observer of the
political world.' As an example of the work,
take this passage as to Mr Gladstone:—'Mr
Gladstone is the uniting band of a political and
moral puzzle, and a very simple puzzle, when
you see how it grew together. He connects the
commercial—even the ultra-commercial — with
the ultra-ecclesiastical element in the state. He
links the school of aristocratic criticism with the
school of democratic progress. He mediates
between "a spirited foreign policy " and the soft
principles of peace or the selfish principles of
the non-intervention party. He cares even
more than trades' unions for the welfare of the
working man ; more than the manufacturers for

the interests of capital ; more for the cause of retrenchment than the most zealous and avowed foes of Government expenditure ; more for the spread of education than the advocates of a compulsory national system ; more for careful constitutional precedent than the Whigs ; and more for the spiritual independence of the Church than the highest Tories. He unites cotton with culture ; Manchester with Oxford ; the deep classical joy over the Italian resurrection and Greek independence with the deep English interest in the amount of the duty on Zante raisins and Italian rags. . . . Mr Gladstone does not sink his rhetorical wells deep. He keeps in the middle region of practical fancy, of applied imagination. . . . These are the influences which seem to us to have made Mr Gladstone what he is, a statesman of the very highest class of the second rank, or, as some one epigrammatically said of him, "a statesman of second-rate intellect in a first-rate state of effervescence," a statesman on whom we could scarcely rely to direct our policy in moments of difficulty, or to sway alone the mind of Parliament, but yet a statesman of far greater power than those who would be competent to guide and lead him, a statesman of wonderful resource on *all* sub-

jects, of fine insight on many, but not a statesman of deeply-matured political principles, nor
one of the safest judgment.'   Mr Hutton, no
doubt, thought more of Mr Gladstone in later
years, and up to the fatal introduction of the
Home Rule policy they were intimate friends.
Even when each took a separate way the *Spectator* remained one of the very few important
journals on the Unionist side, into which crept
none of that cheap criticism of a great man gone
astray which so belittles the critic, and in the
eye of the reader who seeks to ' hold the balance
even,'—to use General Gordon's motto—earns
nothing but contempt.   We may be certain of
this, that had the younger man been allowed to
see the veteran statesman join the majority, no
fairer, more generous, more finely adjusted ap-
praisement of Mr Gladstone at his best and
widest, would have appeared anywhere, than the
one which the *Spectator* of that noteworthy week
would have given to the world.

Lord Beaconsfield was a kind of man Mr
Hutton could ill endure : he was of a sort to
which his critic could perhaps do but scant
justice, although justice was a passion with
him.   All his life he felt the showman side of
the man to be uppermost, and although Lord

Beaconsfield had, no doubt, his better qualities,
these were not in themselves sufficiently all-
pervading to be esteemed even at their pro-
portional values.   It fared so, also, with Lord
Lytton, the first.   Mr Hutton greatly disliked
the grandiose pose of such men, and here again
I think he failed to separate the gold from
the dross, or rather to perceive the presence
of gold at all, his assay being of almost too
harsh a kind.   Indeed, without thinking, I
have used something like his own words when
he said of Lord Beaconsfield :—'Disraeli's showy
gilding will not stand the acid test for gold.'
'It is becoming every day evident,' he continued, 'that he *is* a foreign body in that torpid
organisation [the Conservative party], and will
some day soon be ejected from it in some un-
expected part, as a needle that has been
swallowed years ago will suddenly work out,
not without pain, and gathering, and inflam-
mation, in the fleshy part of the arm, or the
leg, or even at the foot.'   He did not foresee
that whatever Lord Beaconsfield's faults may
have been, and however foreign a body in the
Conservative party he might at that time appear, never would parliamentary chief more successfully grapple his followers to himself, and,—

to carry on the metaphor — cause a single
needle to beget and magnetise needles enough
to join themselves together, and so bind the
disintegrated units of a party as with hoops
of steel.

More interesting, perhaps, in these days, is
the forecasting of the position he expected
Lord Salisbury, then Lord Cranborne, to take.
'Amongst the few Conservatives of the younger
generation,' writes he, ' who have shown marked
ability and capacity for something larger than
Conservative timidities and Tory prejudices,
must be reckoned Lord Cranborne. If he
should remain long enough in the House of
Commons, there is no man more likely to
succeed Mr Disraeli in the leadership of the
Conservative party, or to lead it ably and vigorously, if at times imprudently, than Lord
Cranborne. He always carries war into the
enemy's country, and always does it with
acrimonious ability. Lord Cranborne almost
always speaks as if his mind was fitted with
a false bottom a good deal nearer the surface
than the springs of his thought. The one
class of questions on which he has been really
rash, is that of foreign policy. On foreign
questions where political instinct and feeling

are stronger than reason, he will always be
in danger of yielding to the force of his anti-
pathies. There is no better debater in the
House of Commons than Lord Cranborne.' In
the eyes of later critics, rashness is perhaps the
last political vice the present Prime Minister's
foreign policy suggests.

The other books need not be individually
touched upon. They are much better known.
They present the two supreme interests which
divided their author's life and energies as a
critic, and as a man,—literature and religion.
And yet one feels indisposed to make even
this distinction, for all such separation between
the literary and religious writings of Mr Hutton
is arbitrary, and more or less ineffectual. To
him, indeed, there was but *one* life. To make
much of the religion of a literary man, as
such, would have seemed to him nothing less
than the impertinence it really is. A literary
man may, of course, if he chooses, have his
religion like others ; but he must surely adjust
himself to the creative forces like the rest.
The announcement that he is a literary man
will not terrify the Powers that be, into
giving him special terms. There is a way of
talking about God, as if He should feel more

than usually gratified by the notice a literary man takes of Him. In speaking of William Rufus, Mr Hutton himself said he had a 'way of looking upon God as a sort of Suzerain, from whom, if he had any cause of grievance against Him, his allegiance was to be temporarily withdrawn ;' and many of the *Spectator's* severe references to the German Kaiser for kindred posturing were doubtless from his pen. Anything approaching this kind of thing was absolutely abhorred by Mr Hutton. The religion of a literary man is, after all, apt in its self-complacent account of its own fine qualities, to end in the literary man, pure and simple, leaving the religion to go its way naked as it came. While Mr Hutton would, no doubt, have admitted that good literature of a sort might be made out of bad ethics, it would have grieved him to make the admission ; for he was so interpenetrated with the moral idea, that neither felicity of expression nor daring originality of outlook, blinded him to the fact that true greatness involved in some very deep sense, true goodness. He saw things whole and his vision was singularly sane. To him, indeed, lines of demarcation were not unbroken walls, but light fences, whose use as landmarks he was too wise to question, although he knew well enough how to find his way through them. For present purposes, however, it may be well to divide his literary from his distinctively religious writings.

The two volumes ' On Contemporary Thought and Thinkers,' are reprints from the *Spectator*. The papers are, of course, of the usual length of a leading article in the Wellington Street organ, and cannot thus afford those branchings off into thought — co-related to the subjects under discussion,—so dearly loved by Mr Hutton, and in virtue of which (let the scrappy writer who fancies great questions can be disposed of by a few staccato sentences, which he calls impressions, hug his faith if he will), to the patient reader the full and satisfying view arises. Again and again he returns to his favourite subjects in these books. Merely to turn the pages of the five volumes (leaving, in the meantime, his biographies of Scott and Newman outside the number and survey) is to see for ourselves how dearly he loved to consider Wordsworth, George Eliot, and Matthew Arnold. Let us look at some of his general characteristics as a literary critic—and a great one he certainly was. A writer in the *Speaker*, indeed, tells us that he once heard Mr Gladstone mention Mr Hutton as 'The first critic of the nineteenth century.' Something like the same verdict has, rightly or wrongly, been attributed to Mr Morley. Certainly Mr Morley showed his appreciation of Mr Hutton when he gave him the second of the volumes, which he as general editor was responsible to Messrs Macmillan for, in the 'English Men of Letters' series,— giving the initial volume to Mr Leslie Stephen, a man whose posture towards literature and ethics he must have felt to be very much nearer his own than that of the literary editor of the *Spectator*. It is easy to pooh-pooh Mr Gladstone's statement, but it must be borne in mind that Mr Hutton was much more than a *literary* critic :—he was also a critic of theology and philosophy, as well as politics ; and while many might be inclined to place others above him as literary critics, who else, it may be asked, has played so powerful a part in all of these departments ? It is worth while adding in this connection that when the 'English Leaders of Religion' series came out, it was to him that the general editor of those useful books turned, to supply the public with the first volume.

It is impossible to traverse the large round of criticism that was to the man whose work is being considered, the very breath of his nostrils. Only a general survey of his methods, and a glance at some of the major positions taken up regarding great personalities and their writings may be attempted. A few things may be premised as outstanding : the absolute absence of flippancy ; the sterling qualities of the full rich mind, which the critic brings to bear upon the subjects he places before himself. The expression is used advisedly—they are placed before himself, and not his readers, in the first place. He takes himself and his work always seriously. There is no posing. There is not the slightest attempt to say clever things, although many clever things are said. Indeed, I question whether any such tendency lay in R. H. Hutton's nature, and he need not, perhaps, be credited with fighting a temptation which, virile and insinuating in other literary men's lives, had for him no existence at all. The *Saturday Review* professes to find a ' lady-like order in all his opinions.' But this is surely to miss the mark. A certain orderliness, there no doubt is, but it has sheer strength and robust judgment for its begetters, rather than feminine timidity and primness. It takes some vanity—and we do well to remind ourselves that all vanity is not of the basest sort —to approach great men of letters, or the great creations of their genius, gaily and jauntily as, for example, Matthew Arnold did. Mr Hutton was in truth the least vain of all our great critics,—and I do not think any one who carefully peruses his books will hesitate to apply the adjective to him, certainly not the more because the critic claims so little for himself. It is true there is no absence of decision. When he says ' I believe,' one feels that the words cover a great certainty to him. They have nothing in them of the questioning roll of eye— to see how you are taking it, as it were—which is the mark, for example, of Mr Hall Caine's egotism ; nothing of that prim, self-enjoying contempt, so oddly mixed with thin but genuine pity, which plays about the columnar Ies that plentifully speckle the pages of A. K. H. B., nor yet anything of what may be called the ' big-boy-bumptious' egotism of Mr Crockett, and certain others of our younger novelists, who seem to have no ear for the 'sullen Lethe rolling

doom' on the little brief authority an ephemeral
fame is supposed to confer. There is absolutely
nothing of any of these kinds of egotism about
the 'I' of Mr Hutton. His affirmation stands for
the plain steadfast emphasis of a man who has
earned his convictions by the sweat of his
brow. The personal pronoun is noticeable
neither for its frequency nor its infrequency.
It is there when needed ; not ashamed of itself,
not proud of itself, but absolutely necessary to
itself and to the man who uses it. Take this as
an example from one of his papers on Cardinal
Newman. He is speaking of Newman before
he left the Church of England, when he was
filled with a wistful hope that by his influence
he might (as many other reformers so called,
believe) improve the church from the inside.
For a time he worked away with a 'sad
sincerity,' to use Emerson's phrase. When Mr
Hutton comes to discuss the Cardinal's standpoint, and ask where he went wrong, one feels
that the veneration for Newman is so great that
it bids him pause. No one can read the modest
way in which he expresses his dissent without
feeling the critic become larger because of his
admissions. 'Of course,' writes he, 'one does
not like to say of a man of the highest genius,

and of a kind of genius specially adapted to the subject on which he writes, that he is wrong, and that a man of no genius who criticises him, is right ; but still, as I believe that he did go seriously wrong, and should be a Roman Catholic myself if I did not, I must give my explanation of the error I think I see.' It is Mr Hutton's literary criticism that is before us now, but these words have been quoted because they illustrate better than any others could do the posture of the man. He might have written so of Wordsworth's view of anything, though scarcely of Goethe's or of Matthew Arnold's.

If Mr Hutton had been a lesser man, he might have been a *finer*, but I cannot use the word greater writer, although I fancy many would have no such hesitation. Until a man can honestly say that manner comes before matter in his regard, he will prove his loyalty to the soul of things by letting those who assert this, go their way without his company. Surely whatever the fastidious may see amiss in his style as a writer, as a critic, Mr Hutton deserves well to be remembered. He has not the sudden picturesqueness of Hazlitt, though he has far greater probing powers in many directions. He has not

E

the faintest desire—anyone can see it for himself —to glitter like a brook in the open sunshine. Where his subject takes him he goes. He follows the gleam, like Merlin, and it is no Will o' the Wisp. In imaginative literature, Mr Frederick Greenwood has told us, Mr Hutton demanded 'sanity, sweetness, order, honesty of perfect health,' but there need be no restriction in the application, for these things above all others he looked for everywhere. Like Browning he could truthfully say he had nothing to do 'with the slothful, with the mawkish, the unmanly.' He forges ahead—one naturally uses a verb that pre-supposes an element of density and opposition to move in—like the bows of a sea-going ship that knows her way. It may be, and often is, neces-sary to tack (and the reader who does not notice how he goes back to catch a little wind, or a helpful current, but who takes all the doublings for mere repetitions, is sure to miss much), but give him time and he will arrive. Short cuts are an abomination to him because they are gained so often by transgression of a wise law of trespass, and offer mere speed, as compensation for lost opportunities and points of richer view. I re-member Mr Lang holding up to ridicule, on account of its construction, one long sentence of

Hutton's. I forget what pleasant 'sign' swung over the utterance, but I distinctly recall the language as giving the impression that Mr Lang, with that smile-provoking aloofness of his, had not heard Mr Hutton's name mentioned more than once before. Mr Lang had, no doubt, seized on a faulty passage, but he would surely be among the last to deny the extreme beauty of many sentences of Mr Hutton's if these were placed before him. We must never forget that the chief desire on the part of Mr Hutton was to fully understand the subject-matter of his criticism, and it is evident he knew no haste; believing that 'too fast arrives as tardy as too slow.' I cannot think he fails in any of his more important essays and judgments to make his view a real contribution to the better knowledge of a great writer's work and standpoint. Those who say he is not a lucid writer seem to me to confound lucidity with brevity. It may be worth while dwelling on this point for a moment. Take up almost any one of his articles and it will at once lead you away from the margins of things. But he is a worker with a variety of tools. In other words, as a subject deepens before him, his method of treatment sympathetically evolves an elaboration which none will regret so

much as those whose grasp of the matter
is slack, and whose patience naturally gives in,
while the weight of the body, to use such a
figure, hangs but by a finger or two. Take, for
example, his book of political portraits. To read
these sketches is to find a somewhat easy handling the prevalent method. It is the outstanding general features of the men who appear
before him, that he seeks to catch and render in
a manner fitted to the restricted space of a *Pall
Mall Gazette* column or two. But when the discussion is one that concerns details ; when
every side-light thrown on a complex character
or an ethical problem is felt to demand its due, a
marked difference in presentment arises. It may
be that he erred a little in overvaluing certain
matters, but it must be remembered that so
thorough was his treatment, and so sensitive his
feeling for causes which escape many other people,
that one may well hesitate to describe anything
as an unimportant element, in a criticism that has
so very powerful and satisfying an effect in its com-
pleted form. There is almost a sense of finality
about his best work, from which one rises as from
a full meal. It has been said Mr Hutton went to
the heart of things, but he had, at the same time, a
curious habit of taking a process of reasoning, ap-

plied it may have been to some exalted subject, and bringing it to bear on what seemed an altogether remote and very much less dignified matter. He had not a little of Wordsworth's undersense of greatness in what are called small things. The writer of this monograph remembers the surprise he felt in finding an article he had contributed to one of the reviews, made a text of in the *Spectator* for a disquisition on common sense,—a subject on the face of it, at least, by no means even analogous to his own. Nevertheless the affinity was really there, and with it, of course, the justification of the applied reasoning. In later years, most of Mr Hutton's critics are agreed that what has been called his prolixity grew upon him. It was, however, no mere evil habit. It followed a deliberate primary desire to make his own point plain, and also to anticipate and pre-judge objections that might arise in other minds. But there was a finer and more sensitive feeling still at the root of the matter. There was present a deep-seated wish to persuade, not by the kind of reckless daring that carries conviction by storm into the minds of some, but by a tacit acknowledgment of the increasing difficulties that attend the settlement of many modern questions, followed by a very precise and

authoritative method of helping forward the
decision, not only by referring to the obstacles
themselves, but by, as it were, stooping to remove
them from the path, as one who had himself
known them and suffered because of them.   No
doubt the man was the nobler for the effort,
but the style, so-called, suffered harm thereby.
The language became complex, and, after all,
why not ?—for it concerned itself not so much
with the utterance of one man, as with anticipated
responses of many kinds from many readers.
As the *Pall Mall Gazette* phrased it, ' his sentences went tottering on, bent double under
all their burden of thought.'   In a sense there
can be no doubt his articles became more and
more laboured ;—not that they bore signs of
fatigue or unnecessary workmanship, but in so
far as they were made greater burden-bearers.
He was, as it has been stated, a critic who
always carried heavy guns, and one might add,
that even in the intervals of firing there was an
attendant rumble that told of weight. Listen
to what he himself has to say on the point
of style.   He is discussing Carlyle's language :—
' I say this not without fully recognising that
simplicity is the highest of all qualities of style,
and that no one can pretend to find simplicity

in Carlyle's mature style. But as, after all, the purpose of style is to express thought, if the central and pervading thought which you wish to express, and must express if you are to attain the real object of your life, is inconsistent with simplicity, let simplicity go to the wall, and let us have the real drift.' It is not, however, what may be called the bad art in Hutton, so much as the generous purpose and real but orderly enthusiasm, that one loves to dwell on.

Let us now see what some of his literary verdicts are. His profound admiration for Sir Walter Scott rises to the surface whenever opportunity affords, but one notes that he scarcely separates the man from his works ; that is to say, he believes Scott himself lived the heroic life, and that life it was that, turning its energies into imaginative channels, created for us the long procession of moving men and women, many of whom without thinking too deeply, feel strongly, and act nobly. But what is said of Scott's verse is, one cannot help feeling, applied also, though with evident unwillingness, to his fiction. 'The very quality of his verse,' Mr Hutton writes, 'which makes it seize so powerfully on the imaginations of plain, bold, adventurous men, often makes it hammer

fatiguingly against the brain of those who need
the relief of a widening horizon and a richer
world.' It is this yearning for a wide, ever-
widening horizon that is perhaps the dominant
note of R. H. Hutton's nature. He pursued—
to use his own fine phrase—'the ever-retreating
horizon of eternal life.' He has described the
published life of Maurice as appearing neces-
sarily 'the story of a shadow in a dream' in
the eyes of such as think there is no eternal
world; and it is not too much to say, that
although he himself had, as a journalist, to
pass comment on all manner of things, his
criticism never stopped short with the seen
and apparent. As a writer in the *Times* truly,
if a little laboriously, put it: 'It was as if
within the folds of the long-drawn sinuous
complex involutions of a style never swift,
sometimes prolix and toilsome, there were a
subtle aroma; something not felt by the
uninitiated was there to satisfy and refresh
certain minds in their trouble. . . . He was at
his best when with delicacy and subtlety he
gave shape and intellectual cogency to what
in others were aspirations, vague, unsatisfied
desires, when by stating and restating, touch
upon touch, he at last laboriously but perfectly

visualised that which had flashed mistily a
penumbra before some baffled searcher after
truth.' No doubt these words apply more
specifically to his religious writings, but they
cover all his work. Hence one is prepared to
believe that in natures which sought distant
horizons he found his best companionship. It
was not necessary that the horizons should be
rosy, as witness his love of Matthew Arnold,
notwithstanding that great poet's chill October
light ; and of George Eliot, in spite of her
determination to live without opium, as she
called the effort, which she assiduously cultivated,
of dropping hope after hope out of her life. To
supremely interest Hutton, a writer required
to be one with whom the burden of the mystery
of all this unintelligible world was profoundly
present. Whether some serene or blessed mood
was gained, which lightened the burden, or there
arrived only — what Hazlitt once described
Wordsworth's Laodamia as having,—' the sweetness, the gravity, the strength, the beauty, and
the languor of death,' he was imaginatively
present. I say *imaginatively* present, because he
himself—as we shall see later on—had taken
deeper soundings and held with Tennyson, that,
in spite of appearances, ' All is well ! ' But it

was in his nature to delight in setting opposites
fairly and squarely against each other, and no
one hated more thoroughly than he did (as his
paper, for example, on 'The Hard Church'
proves) that style of criticism which makes
difference of standpoint between the critic and
the mind criticised, an excuse for giving little or
no consideration to the processes which lead to
the parting of the ways. The unknown made
infinite and habitual appeal to him, but he was
none the less one who yet retained—

> 'The warm touch of the world that lies to hand,
> Not in vague dreams of man forgetting man,
> Nor in vast morrows losing the to-day;
> Who trusted nature, trusted fate, nor found
> An ogre, sovereign on the throne of things;
> Who felt the incumbence of the unknown, yet bore
> Without resentment the Divine reserve.'

His volume of 'Literary Essays' concerns
itself wholly, with one exception, with poets and
poetry. That exception is a finely discriminating paper on Hawthorne, who was, he considered, as a literary artist, if not in mere rough
genius, almost the first, and quite the highest
fruit of American culture. The essays deal
with Goethe, Wordsworth, Shelley, Arnold,
Browning, Tennyson, and others. The paper

on Goethe is an extraordinarily able piece of criticism. It is in no spirit of profound adoration—as was Carlyle's habitual posture—that he approaches the great German ; nor is it, one need hardly add, in a spirit of carping criticism on the other hand. The essay is a calm, judicial, weighty review of the life and works of Goethe. In speaking of the poet's detachment—to use a word in vogue—Hutton aptly likens him to the little three-eyed girl in the German tale. He had 'always an extra organ besides the eyes he slept and wept with, to take note of his own sleep and his own tears, and an extra will, subject to the command of the third eye, ready to rescue the ordinary will from the intricacies of human emotion.' It is by no means easy to forget such a picture as this. The manner in which Goethe at first repels English readers with English views of life and duty, and afterwards, as it were, mesmerises them until they feel his proud aloofness from much that has hitherto been absolutely needful to them, drawing them to himself, is admirably described. There is something keenly accurate in the observation that in the Weimar giant's eyes, religion was 'not the communion with holiness, but at most, a graceful development of human life, a fountain of cool mystery

playing gratefully on a parched earth.' Any
one of whom this might truly be said, could
never fascinate a man like Hutton even by
mesmerism.   Newman, Maurice, Dr James
Martineau, drew him by a deeper and subtler
charm.   At the same time he was much too
great a critic to allow the recognition of what
must have been to him a profoundly radical
defect, to influence his view of the poet's literary
splendour.   He makes fun of the mass of comment which, after the manner of German criticism, every action and poem has given rise to.
The Frederika episode is thus commented on :—
'Frederika . . . little knew . . . that a very
ponderous "Frederike litteratur" would arise, in
which an erudition, as yet unborn, would discuss
with prodigious learning and subtlety, after
collation of MS. letters, personal examination of
the place and cross-questioning of aged survivors,
the precise point where Goethe had crossed the
Sesenheim Road, the position of Frederika's own
parlour, the date of the first kisses she bestowed.'
Mr Hutton thinks that the miserable dream of
keeping the course of Goethe's inward development free from all foreign interference had much
to answer for.   Goethe's own words are these :—
'The desire to raise the pyramid of my exist-

ence—the base of which is already laid—as high
as possible in the air absorbs every other desire,
and scarcely ever quits me;' upon which Hutton
frankly comments :—' To have loved the goodness
of either God or man more devotedly than he
loved its reflex image in his own character,
would have done him more good than all the
sickly pottering with the " pyramid of his existence " with which he was so much occupied.' As
for Goethe's loves (and we all know Goethe loved
much—and many) his critic acutely remarks,
' He wished for love with limited liability,' and
pokes fun at an as yet unaccomplished task of
the German commentators, which might take
the form of a distinct classification of Goethe's
sweethearts. These, he thinks, might be said to
consist of about 8 Al's ; 5 at least Æl's, and
finally a great number of ' holde Wesen,' some
of them ' already obscured by the shadows of
time,' who were ' the recipients of a more
transient adoration.' Notwithstanding a great
deal of iconoclasm, the essay shows the writer
to have been not at all insensible to the mys-
terious simplicity of Goethe's best work. His
lyrics he held to be perfect—escaping ' as un-
consciously from the essence of the earth and
air as the scent from a violet, or the music

from a bird.' In the man himself, he recog-
nises 'great generosity,' (for Goethe gave away
one-sixth of his income in charity without letting
his left hand know what his right hand did,) and
lauds him for much else, but finally regards him
as 'perhaps the wisest man totally without moral
humility and personal faith whom the world has
ever seen.' A noble ending is made to a noble
essay in these words :—' And so, with his eyes
still clinging to the life he left, on the 22nd
March 1832, he passed away himself, while drawing with his finger pictures in the air and mur-
muring a last cry for " more light." During the
years which have intervened, the influence of
his writings in England has steadily increased.
He has been held up as the wisest man of modern
days, and by some half-worshipped as a demigod.
And in truth, his was a light and spacious mind.
I grant that he was the wisest man of modern
days who ever lacked the wisdom of a child ;
the deepest who never knew what it was to
kneel in the dust with bowed head and broken
heart. And he was a demigod, if a demigod be a
being at once more and less than ordinary men,
having a power which few attain, and owing
it, in part, to a deficiency in qualities in which
few are so deficient ; a being who puts forth a

stronger fascination over the earth because
expending none of his strength in yearnings
towards heaven.   In this sense Goethe was a
demigod :—

> " He took the suffering human race ;
>   He read each wound, each weakness, clear ;
>   He struck his finger on the place,
>   And said, ' Thou ailest here and here.' "

He knew all symptoms of disease, a few allevia-
tions, no remedies.   The earth was eloquent to
him, but the skies were silent.   Next to Luther
he was the greatest of the Germans ; next—but
what a gulf between !   "Adequate to himself,"
was written on that broad, calm forehead ; and
therefore men thronged eagerly about him to
learn the incommunicable secret.   It was not
told, and will not be told.   For man it is a
weary way to God, but a wearier far to any
demigod.'   So ends what Professor Henry
Drummond, greatly daring, called 'the best
critical piece that had been written in this
century.'

It were out of place to dwell at length on
the admirable papers on Wordsworth and the
rest.   No reader of the *Spectator* need be told—
and the editor's own papers on such subjects

were easily recognised—how fondly Wordsworth
was regarded.   I know of no other critic
who has so felicitously summed up Wordsworth's superb qualities, and I do not forget
Mr Frederic Myers's name in this connection.
Take one passage as an example of many :—
' There is no other great poet who thus redeems
new ground for spiritual meditation from beneath the very sweep of the tides of the most
engrossing affections, and quietly maintains it
in possession of the musing intellect.   There is
no other but Wordsworth who has led us to
those sweet counsels between head and heart
which flash upon the absorbing emotions of the
moment the steady light of a calm infinite
world.   None but Wordsworth has ever so
completely transmuted by an imaginative spirit
unsatisfied yearnings into eternal truth.' He
was not indeed unaware of Wordsworth's weaknesses, for he describes the poet as a blind man
kindling his own fire, lighting it often without
seeing that the fuel was damp and could not
catch a spark ; and thus though he has left us,—
again I quote Mr Hutton's own words,—'Many
a beacon of pure and everlasting glory flaming
from the hills, he has left us also many a monu-
mental pile of fuel from which the poetic fire

has early died away.' From Wordsworth to Shelley is a considerable leap, but we find the paper on the latter full of pregnant and search-ing criticism. He held that Shelley's lyrics, for example—and few who know them will deny the truth of the statement—'seem fuller of spiritual fire than any other English poet has poured into our language.' How much freedom, and beauty, and truth, lie in such a statement as this : ' His [Shelley's] poetry is the poetry of desire. He is ever the *homo desideriorum :* always thirsting, always yearning ; never pour-ing forth strains of a thankful satisfaction, but either the cravings of an expectant rapture, or the agony of a severed nerve. This is the great distinction which separates him from the other poetical mystics of his day. Wordsworth, for instance, is always exulting in the fulness of nature ; Shelley always chasing fallen stars. Wordsworth gratefully pierces the homely crust of earth to find the rich fountains of life in the Eternal mind ; Shelley follows with wistful eye the fleeting stream of beauty as it for ever escapes him into the illimitable void.' Brown-ing, he believed, had the keenest of all eyes for everything that altered the point of view, but was, nevertheless, never really dramatic, for he

F

failed to hide from us his own critical eye, and
was continually tossing thoughts and impressions
about, with here and there touches of sarcasm and
caricature, in a manner that declared plainly he
was looking *into* the situation, not looking out
from the *inside*.   Could any picture more accu-
rately represent the concentrated force of
Browning's utterance than that in which the
poet is seen directing a stream of thought
pointedly through 'a sort of intellectual hose
on a specific object.'   It is playfully observed
that many of Browning's poems must have been
written solely for the benefit of the Browning
Society and not for mankind in general.   All
the while, however, Mr Hutton plainly indicates
that, in his opinion, Browning's range of thought
placed him far above most of his poetic contem-
poraries ; while his vividness of conception gave
him a position second to none but Tennyson.
Lord Tennyson himself—who, along with Arnold,
is said to have confessed his obligation to R. H.
Hutton for his powerful and sympathetic criticism—he held to be one of the greatest masters
of metre, both simple and sonorous, that the
English language has ever known.   He is
keenly discriminating in separating the noble
poetry in Tennyson's work from what he calls

the 'falsetto.' There is, he thinks, hardly finer
reflective poetry in existence than much of
Tennyson's at its best. Of the picture of the
dawn, which occurs towards the end of 'In
Memoriam,' he writes with infectious enthusiasm : 'I know no descriptive poetry that has
the delicate spiritual genius of that passage, its
sweet mystery, its subdued lustre, its living
truth, its rapture of peace. And besides the
indescribable beauty of the pictures in "In
Memoriam," in intellectual depth, especially in
the truthfulness of its knowledge of the heart,
and in the elasticity of soul which thrusts back
the heaviest burdens by its own inherent force,
this poem has never been rivalled in its kind by
any English poet.' 'The Idylls of the King'
has rarely been so keenly scrutinised—and many
microscopes have been focussed over it. As a
result of the analysis, the book has, perhaps,
never found so powerful a special pleader
as it has in Mr Hutton. Room must be
found for one passage on the subject. 'If
not,' writes he, 'the most perfectly finished of
Tennyson's poems, "The Idylls of the King"
has a grander aim and larger scope than any,
and paints the waste places of the heart and the
strength of the naked soul with a stronger and

more nervous touch.   As the rich colours of the great story fade, the air fills with low spiritual rumours of that higher life of which the Order of the Round Table is but a symbol; while Tennyson paints the stately passing of the spirit to its rest as he painted the greatness of its rising, but with added touches of mystery and beauty.   The old Arthurian epic has been rendered by Tennyson significant to modern ears.   In it he has found the common term between the ideas of chivalry, and the ideas of an age of hesitating trust, an age of a probing intellect and of a trusting heart.   The conquests and the yearnings, and the sad resolves of a spirit far too kingly to rule successfully men who only half recognise the kingly voice, have never before been delineated by a poet who can use almost all the wealth of colour belonging at once to the visible and the invisible life, with the reticent hand and sure eye of Tennyson's rich and patient and spiritual genius.'   I think it will be admitted that this description is as true as it is exquisitely worded.

The 'imperious serenity' of Matthew Arnold exercised a strange kind of spell over Hutton, who had not, after all, a very great deal in

common with that poet. Much of the senti-
ment, he frankly admits, runs counter to his
own deepest convictions. Nevertheless he
greatly appreciated Arnold's scholarly delicacy
and simplicity of touch. He has indeed taken
leave to doubt whether one awkward or turgid
word occurs in any of Arnold's poems, but goes
back upon himself to make an exception of the
word 'pullulating,' which occurs in the poem
on Dean Stanley. Thinness is the last attribute
to be applied to Mr Hutton's criticism, and
only a critic of an exceptionally high order
could sum up so powerfully and truthfully the
essence of Arnold's poetry : ' When I come to
ask,' writes he, 'what Mr Arnold's poetry has
done for this generation, the answer must be
that no one has expressed more powerfully and
poetically its spiritual weaknesses, its craving
for a passion that it cannot feel, its admiration
for a self-mastery that it cannot achieve, its
desire for a creed that it fails to accept, its
sympathy for a peace that it does not know.'
What keen insight too lies in the conclusion
he reaches, that there was always a tincture of
pride — which was anything but silent — in
Arnold's confessions that he was unable to
believe,—accompanied as these were with a self-

congratulation that he was too knowing to yield
to the temptations of his heart! The great
qualities of Arnold's poetry are thus sum-
marised at the close of a singularly fine piece
of criticism : ' As the poet of the soul's melancholy hauteur and plaintive benignity, as the
exponent of pity for the great excess of her
wants beyond her gifts and graces, as the singer
at once of the spirit's hunger, of the insuffi-
ciency of the food which the intellect provides
for her cravings, and yet also of her fastidious
rejection of more heavenly nutriment, Mr
Arnold will be read and remembered by every
generation in which faith continues to be
daunted by reason, and reason to seek, not
without pangs of inexplicable compunction to
call in question the transcendental certainties
of faith.'

It will be seen that we are dealing with a
critic of an order which the large class of
worshippers, whose expressed views of their
favourites are wholly one-sided, may not readily
take kindly to : but can there be such a thing
as sound criticism at all, unless there is frankness,
and freedom, and insight, as well as charity,
enthusiasm, appreciation ? Mr Ruskin is, no
doubt, a great critic, but surely this description

of Turner cannot be called great criticism : 'He is the epitome of all art, the concentration of all power ; there is nothing that ever artist was ever celebrated for that he cannot do better than the most celebrated. He seems to have seen everything in the visible world ; there is nothing he has not done, nothing that he dares not do.' One never comes on anything of this sort in Hutton—who, by the way, has called Ruskin 'the most delicate and eloquent writer on the beauty of nature and art that England has ever known.' There is, however, one great simi- larity, if no other, between the two men. It was said of Mr Ruskin, in the *Daily News* the other day, on the occasion of his having reached his eightieth birthday, that 'no reward, no honour or recognition have ever had a place in his scheme of providence.' These words equally apply to Mr Hutton. One does not forget that the *Spectator* has become an excellent property ; but this success has come as a matter of course ; certainly not because the journal has swerved, as not a few others have done, this way and that, to catch money, as a clown catches on his head his tossed-up fool's cap. There was no species of bribery that found Mr Hutton vulnerable. He went his way clad, as

Alexander Smith puts it, 'in the armour of a pure intent.' He was full of insight, generosity, severity. He was, at the same time, more free from malice than any outstanding critic of his time, and he was absolutely—if one may use the word regarding mortal man — without hypocrisy.

One is glad to see the announcement * that Miss Roscoe is to publish another volume of her uncle's shorter criticisms, of which two volumes, selected from the *Spectator*, and known as 'Criticisms on Contemporary Thought and Thinkers,' have already been printed. These have the same strong qualities as the longer essays, but space makes compression more necessary, and the style suffers. It can never have been an easy thing for Hutton to let a subject go. Of padding there is none, of packing there is enough and to spare. Among

---

* The volume referred to has, since the above lines were written, been sent out as one of Messrs Macmillan & Co.'s well-known 'Eversley' series under the title of 'Aspects of Religious and Scientific Thought.' It will be prized for its fifty-four *Spectator* articles, which are characterised by the same great variety, rich suggestiveness, and strength of handling, that mark 'Criticisms on Contemporary Thought and Thinkers.' The book is embellished with an admirable portrait,—a welcome addition which, however, could not have been looked for had Mr Hutton been still amongst us.

the more interesting of these criticisms are
the fine outspoken papers on Carlyle. There
is, as might be expected, a good deal of
trenchant criticism,—Carlyle's literary motive
power being regarded by his critic, more
as 'a humorous wonder than a moral
passion.'

Mr Hutton had no love of screaming. He
never screamed himself, and he cared little for
the uplifted voice : to deepen an impression
he would himself naturally have lowered his
own. Nowise blind to Carlyle's greatness (he
calls him, indeed, the world's greatest painter
of the interior life of man), he, nevertheless, regards him as one whose own interior
life, as it appears in his private diaries, had
the unenviable distinction of possessing a
semi-artificial manner, which suggests a con-
sciousness of audience. It goes without saying
that Scott is championed in the face of
Carlyle's ill-natured and ill-inspired attacks
'Where in the world could Carlyle,' cries he,
'have found nobler evidences of the higher
standard of worth than in the works of the
great genius of his age, Sir Walter Scott . . .
for if ever there were a man whose writings
showed a profound appreciation of moral worth

as distinct from conventional worth, it was Sir
Walter Scott.' A much lengthier essay on
Carlyle, however, appears in 'Essays on some
of the Modern Guides to English Thought in
matters of faith,' and in this he tries to show—
and one is bound to admit he does not fail—
that the great organs of destruction are more
esteemed by Carlyle, than the constructive
forces. He speaks of Carlyle's sympathy with
Cromwell, Frederick, Mirabeau, Danton, and
even Goethe, in what they destroyed rather
than in that which they built up ; and with a
clean sweep of the knife he divides what may
be called Carlyle's moral, from his intellectual,
benefits to the race. While showing how he
despised all of positive in the political and
philanthropical drift of his time ; felt but little
interest in science or art ; looked with contempt
on modern religious instructors ; and was, therefore, hardly seriously listened to in such con-
nections, Hutton is not afraid to call the
'French Revolution' one of the most wonderful, though historically least reliable, of the
world's books ; and he expresses his belief that
its author was by far 'the greatest interpreter
our literature has ever had, of the infinite forces
working through society, of that vast dim back-

ground of social beliefs, unbeliefs, enthusiasms, sentimentalities, superstitions, hopes, fears, and trusts, which go to make up either the strong cement or the destructive lava-stream of national life.' It is impossible to read without a smile Hutton's description of the Carlylese we often come upon in Carlyle's work, as something which by its mere force almost persuades one to begin to think that 'a true man should keep his intellect foaming and gasping, as it were, in one eternal epileptic fit of wonder.' Now and again, there can be little doubt, Carlyle is over-severely treated by his critic.

I should have liked to have said something of Mr Hutton's study of George Eliot, which one writer has not hesitated to call 'perhaps the best existing appreciation of that authoress,' but it is impossible. One might linger long enough over many of these fresh and fascinating papers, which are full of variety ; covering criticisms of Dr James Martineau, Ruskin, Dean Stanley, Darwin, Lord Houghton, Dean Church, 'Robert Elsemere,' Huxley, Professor Clifford, Renan, John Stuart Mill, Dickens, Emerson and others.

A large proportion of the criticism, it will have been seen, is concerned with poetry, and one naturally asks the question, whether the critic himself ever seriously sought the muse. He has certainly never asked the public verdict on any such productions of his own, if such there be, but one may, at least, point out that in his powerful essay on 'Goethe and his Influence,' he has given us, half unwillingly, as it were, his own translation of the exquisite little song of Clärchen in 'Egmont,' and other lyrics. One is, however, tempted to go a step farther and see Hutton's own hand in the lines entitled 'The Roseg at Midnight,' which are passed on to the readers of 'Holiday Rambles' as the work of the poetic youth called 'Mr Q.', who, I cannot help thinking, is to be identified with Mr Hutton as surely as the Paul Fleming of 'Hyperion' and the Albano of 'Titan' are to be identified with their creators. The poem is prefaced with the words : 'You must know the Roseg Glacier is dotted with black rocks in grotesque shapes.' It is well worth reproducing here :—

THE ROSEG AT MIDNIGHT

Through the sweet night half waking I had lain,
    Lulled by the murmur of the rushing Inn,
Which seemed like memory without its pain,
    The eager years of youth without their sin.

I rise : in moonlit curves the glacier spreads,
  The peaks in ghostly beauty veil their might,
The dark firs wave their faintly-lighted heads,
  The landscape seems a phantom of the night.

Those polar snows, lapped in soft summer air,
  That ice, which sparkles back a southern moon,
Those black-stoled rocks like monks in wrath or prayer,
  Bowed, bare-kneed, on the glacier, late and soon.

Real are they? or such dreams of fevered brain,
  As wise men conjure now from sky and sod,—
That Love shrinks back from Law's advancing reign,—
  That the Ice-Sea of Science threatens God!'

If the late editor of the *Spectator* was not responsible for these lines, the 'poetic youth, Mr Q.' must, at all events, have occupied a stool at the master's feet.

CHAPTER IV

RELIGION

' OFTEN a cause seems to decline as its champion grows in years, and to die in his death ; but this is to judge hastily; others are destined to complete what he began. No man is given to see his work through. " Man goeth forth unto his work and to his labour until the evening," but the evening falls before it is done. There was One alone who began, and finished, and died.'

JOHN HENRY NEWMAN.

CHAPTER IV

No account of Richard Holt Hutton's books would have anything like the shadow of completeness, that contented itself with viewing their writer merely from the literary side. His nature was profoundly a religious one, and the critic who described him as 'A Stickit Minister,' frankly admits that, from the rostrum of the *Spectator*, 'he preached to a great and listening and picked audience until he died.' I have already said that if you lift up any of Hutton's papers you will be rapidly taken away from the margins of things ; and as all roads were said to lead to Rome, so, no matter where his subjects may have found their beginnings, they turned in time with new emphasis in the direction of eternal life,—using the expression in its first and last of senses.

It was rumoured again and again, during his

G

later years, that Mr Hutton was about to join the
Roman communion, but these tidings all proved
false.   The fact is, he was so eclectic that he could
warmly express himself concerning many things,
which seemed to be in so direct a conflict with
each other that people of another sort were apt
to draw the most unwarrantable conclusions
from his words.   The present writer has, he
believes, read carefully every word of the books
under review,—which run to, at least, nine
volumes,—and while neither he nor any other
reader can fail to see that a church with a
history, a potency, and a refuge from doubt,
such as the Roman Communion affords, was
bound to exercise a certain fascination over such
a mind as Hutton's, there is no single passage
which, while it seems to praise much, has not
its counterpart in another that strikes a note of
warning and condemnation.   His book on
Cardinal Newman—whom he passionately ad-
mired ; and who, in his turn, wrote of Mr
Hutton in 1884, 'I have now for twenty years
held him as a journalist to be a good friend of
mine '—is of comparatively recent date (the proofs
of thè book, indeed, were in its author's hands
when tidings of Newman's death on 11th
August 1890, reached him) and in its pages we

find explicit statement that although he cannot himself fix on any man in England to rival the Cardinal in singleness, devotion, steadfastness, and in the nobility of his main effort in life, he 'cannot adopt Newman's later conceptions of the Church of Christ, hardly even that earlier conception which led so inevitably to the later.' Again, in the chapter on 'Development of Christian Doctrine' in the same book, Newman is taken to task for lecturing on 'The Religious Character of Catholic Countries no Prejudice to the Sanctity of the Church.' Hutton had too free a vision to yield to this obliquity, and writes :—'I should have thought that Christ not only taught that "If any man will do His will, he shall know of the doctrine whether it be of God or whether I speak of myself," but also implied the converse, namely, "If any man will not do His will he shall cease to know of the doctrine whether it be of God or not." At all events, I cannot help thinking that the state of a population absolutely believing in sacred truths which they openly disregard is even more morally hopeless than that of a population which has gradually lost faith in the truths it has practically ignored.' These are not the words of a man on the borders of Roman

Catholicism, but of one who knows by heart the great heritage of good, common to all good men, yet who also knows the evils which he would restrict to the few, if not, indeed, eliminate from all. Hence, although he could go the length of saying, when he describes the Cardinal's entrance into the Roman Catholic Church : 'The long gestation was accomplished, and Newman was born into the communion of the one Christian Church which has a historical continuity and an external organisation as impressive and conspicuous as even his heart could desire for the depository of revealed truth,' he could also speak of the doctrine of the Immaculate Conception as discoursed upon by Newman as something that 'thoroughly bewilders the Protestant imagination beyond anything,' and could describe the fact that the Church shows such avidity in accepting as facts what are merely devotional dreams as the most suspicious of all the aspects of Roman Catholicism.   Again, when discussing Cardinal Newman's 'Lectures on Anglican Difficulties,' Hutton complains that they did not deal at all with what he regards as the greatest of all objections to the Roman Catholic Church, namely, the indifference that Church shows to reasonable criticisms.   The system that not only winked at, but commanded the turning down of the light of reason to a blue peep, so to speak, could never, whatever else of good it included, commend itself to him. It was no light matter in his eyes, to be looked to or forgotten as one went one's ecclesiastical way, that the sanction of the Church was given to utterly unhistorical facts in the Feast of the Assumption of the Virgin Mary, and to the doctrine of the plenary inspiration of the Scriptures. In his essay on the Cardinal in 'Modern Guides of English Thought in Matters of Faith,' when summing up what it was that kept Newman so long from the Roman Communion, he interjects the expressive phrase, 'I wish it had kept him permanently.' That he, notwithstanding all this, resented reference being made to the Roman Catholic Church as a fold for none but silly people, we gather from his stern rebuke to Sir Walter Scott for so thinking. The truth is, Mr Hutton feared nothing in the way of honest assertion. He had no shibboleth of orthodoxy to confront him ; nor had he any of that contemptible vanity that glories in mere heresy as such. He sought *truth*. In a review of Mr John Morley's 'On Compromise,' he confesses that.

he is 'not ashamed to feel far more sympathy
with the nobler aspects of unbelief than
with the ignobler and shiftier aspects of so-
called faith.' He had no more fear of Roman
Catholicism than Mr Balfour has—and we know
that the latter only the other day stated his
belief, that the Protestantism of England was as
unassailable as the law of gravitation. In 1876
Hutton wrote : 'I have none of the horror of
Romanism, as we now know it in England,
which some Protestants seem to think it a kind
of historic duty to feel.' He was, in fact, a
Unitarian who passed with stress and struggle,
as Coleridge did before him, to the Trinitarian
standpoint. He tells us in the preface to the
first edition of his 'Theological Essays' (some of
which papers were reprinted from the old
National Review, though certainly not all of
them, as the *British Weekly* stated some
time ago) that he owed to Mr Maurice,—of
whom he has written at length and with characteristic generosity and fidelity,—more than to
any other man, his belief that theology is a true
science, that a knowledge of God in a true
scientific sense, however imperfect in degree,
is open to us. He had a relentless dislike to
many dogmas, although he remained an attached

member of the Church of England to the last.
Unlike many whose opinions undergo violent
or radical change, there was in the man, beneath
all else, a fine reliable robustness of character
which was not subject to the same change ; a
certain continuity of high principle which went
sounding as an undertone on no 'dim and
perilous way,' while the overtones of thought
seemed possessed of much more freedom, but
had, perhaps, even less power of impressing
minds that fell under his sway. 'Amid all the
perplexities of life' (wrote a sympathetic critic in
the *Westminster Gazette*) 'he was able to main-
tain a clear vision ; and it was this faculty,
coupled with his sterling honesty, his earnestness, his sincerity, that accounted for his great
influence.'

There were certain things he saw very
clearly, and he was not given to affirming too
much when he was not quite sure. He felt
profoundly — and his Unitarianism had helped
him to the view—that a thing is not divine
because we call it so. He knew that it acknowledges no fleeting jurisdiction of ours. He was
also well assured that we are not divine enough
to measure, although we may *feel* its divinity—
not one of us being perfect, no, not even the

youngest of us, as some one has wittily said.
He believed that we become in some sense
divine when the heart in us responds to the
outer appeal, and the inner sanction of the soul
is given. In taking such a view he was, of
course, well aware that the appeal may be
thwarted by the mental and moral cataract that
descends over the unused organ of vision; and
that the awakening which follows the inner
sanction, may lapse into easy drowsiness before it
has well gathered energy of movement; or
again, may find its struggle to obey the high
behest retarded by obstacles which are simply
overwhelming. The great fact that we are
held, rather than that we hold, remained; and
the fact also that our meagre description of
the holding can never be commensurate with
the holding itself. Thus the Trinitarian may
outline his creed as he chooses; it may be filled
with the Divine so far as verbal statement is
concerned, but the channels which should allow
the warm blood currents of the soul to flow
between thinking, feeling, and doing, may be
frozen mid-way. A dogmatical profession of
Unitarianism, on the other hand, he felt to be
not inconsistent with the presence of clear
inlets to the soul, through which 'divine in-

fluence' (a phrase that has been much spoiled in the using) may flow; so that while the mental analysis, so called, results in the expression of a firm negative, the deeper being has, with liberal abandonment, appropriated the finer essence of the spirit of life, and has in doing so gained a larger share of the Christ than those who can name Him and at the same time forget Him,—nay, even with infinite politeness, show Him to the door. Salvation of the soul, he clearly saw, meant not assent merely but consent; meant that the good in us responds to the Best; that sympathies rich and noble become richer and nobler as they rise to meet the Divine, requiring no interpreter, no intermediary,—being themselves, whether they know it or not, children of the Highest! 'As a rule,' Mr Hutton has stated, 'the most depressing and disheartening of all religious literature is the apologetic literature.' As many others have done before him, he has put the matter thus :—'If I wished to doubt the possibility of a revelation I should take a course of reading in defence of it.' Nevertheless his own essay on 'Christian Evidences' is a masterly production, and one might very well hazard one's own spiritual health, by making a careful study of it. It proceeds along inside lines of evidence. Dogma, he considered essential only to display and safeguard revelation, not being itself in any sense *the* revelation. He believed in what are called miracles, although he did not believe that they are, or could be, 'suspensions of natural law,' but only modifications of the results of those laws caused by the introduction into the agencies at work of the influence of controlling spirits of unusual power. He seemed, in fact, even disposed to believe in some modern miracles, so called, and held it to be one of the superstitions of modern science, to ignore that miracles have happened in all ages. We must not forget in this connection that he was a member of the Society for Psychical Research.

Systematised theology he had a great distrust of, being of opinion that when Rome professes to make her survey and map of divine mysteries complete, she falls into the same error as the Scotch Presbyterians ; these last words are his very own, not mine. The evangelical doctrine of justification by faith, as it is generally believed, he contested strongly ; holding that man is and can only be *made* just, not *accounted* just through his faith. The latter view he does not hesitate to call a 'horrible doctrine.' He re-

1 RELIGION

the Holy Spirit,' and only secondarily as the
embodiment of a spirit of true doctrine. He
fortified his large belief in what he called spiritual guidance, by recalling to mind that Socrates
made mention of the guidance of a spirit ; Marcus
Aurelius of the guidance of the divine spirit ; the
Hebrew prophets of the guidance of Jehovah ;
Christ of the guidance of His Father ; the
Apostles of the guidance of the Holy Spirit ;
while Catholics in all ages have spoken of the
guidance of Saints ; Protestants of the guidance
of conscience or of God ; and even Pantheists,
like Renan, he asserted, after giving up belief
in voluntary guidance, believed in that
somewhat groping 'spirit of the whole,' which
the brilliant Frenchman likened to the movement of an oyster or a polype. The intellect,
Hutton held, should be emancipated from what
he called the purely literary superstition as to
the infallibility of the book we call the Bible,
as well as from the belief in an infallible
Church.' 'Every step in the history of
dogmatic orthodoxy,' he writes, 'has been
in effect to justify some reliable human base
for a divine infallibility,' to slide what he describes as a false bottom into the abyss of

Eternal Truth. Coming to his views of Christ,
it is clear, especially from his essay called 'The
Incarnation and Principles of Evidence,' that
his departure from the Unitarian standpoint was
of no wavering kind, but one of the most pronounced and permanent nature. Not only so,
but one feels that he laid himself under obligation to do all he could to overthrow the belief
in which he tells us he was educated, and which
he subsequently endorsed from conviction during many years of anxious thought and study.
He states in as many words that he by-and-bye
accepted the Incarnation as the central truth of
Christian Revelation. It was no mere dull
acceptance, but one that thrilled him with new
life. In an article on 'Creeds and Worship,' he
writes :—'The man who has been wandering by
night upon the mountains does not recall and
describe with a gladder heart the first glimpse
which dawn gave him of the track he had lost,
than that with which one who has found or
recovered his faith in the divine government of
the world and its perfect manifestation in Christ
recites, if he can, the words, 'God of God, Light
of Light, very God of very God.' When this is
said, it does not follow that he held what are
known as strictly orthodox views on the point.

As regards Christ's birth, a correspondent of a
religious newspaper has stated, that he has the
highest authority for saying that Mr Hutton did
not believe in the supernatural coming of Jesus.
Certainly the present writer has failed to
find the ordinary belief explicitly stated anywhere in his writings, while it may be added
that the contention of the correspondent referred to (who, in all likelihood, had other
sources of information than the printed page)
may be borne out by two passages in Mr
Hutton's Life of Newman. He speaks of what
he calls carefully the 'apparent' prediction of a
supernatural birth, and makes haste to add, 'that
is a point on which the best modern Hebrew
scholars are very doubtful;' and, again, it may
be noted, he suggestively interjects an 'if' in
the same connection a little later. But if this
is so, his belief in what is called the divinity of
Christ is none the less a strongly pronounced
one. Christ,' he says in effect, could not have
revealed God without being divine ; and it need
hardly be added, he was not one who could
lightly pass over to the belief, either that Jesus
was an impostor or a self-deluded man. He was
convinced *heartily*—the word is his own—of the
resurrection of Christ. He speaks slightingly,

however, of the 'forensic view' of the atonement, even venturing to use so strong an expression as 'the falsehood of the vicarious theory.' Certain methods of preaching he held in great abhorrence. He regarded, for example, with dislike and distrust, modern revivalist teaching, although, it may be remembered, he thought it worth while to write an article on 'The Metaphysics of Conversion.' The intensity of his veneration and love for Jesus Christ is seen in such a warm burst of feeling as this: 'I never hear without the thrill of a new surprise that calm, strange and unique prophecy addressed at the outset of His short career, to a dozen peasants, "Fear not, little flock, it is your Father's good pleasure to give you the Kingdom," when I remember that a kingdom has really been given to them, though not a kingdom of this world.' Elsewhere he wrote :—

'To me the most touching and satisfying words that have ever been uttered by human lips are those which no mere man could ever have uttered without jarring every chord in the human conscience.

.   .   .   .

'At that time Jesus answered and said, I thank thee, O Father, Lord of heaven and earth, because thou hast hid these things from the wise and prudent, and hast revealed

them to babes : even so, Father, for so it seemed good in thy
sight.   All things are delivered unto me by my Father;
and no man knoweth the Son but the Father; neither
knoweth any man the Father, save the Son, and he to
whomsoever the Son will reveal him.   Come unto me, all
ye that labour and are heavy laden and I will give you rest.
Take my yoke upon you, and learn of me, for I am meek
and lowly in heart, and ye shall find rest unto your souls :
for my yoke is easy and my burden is light.'

Augustine, it is true, made a similar statement fifteen centuries before Mr Hutton wrote
these words, and thousands—comprising the
very flower of humanity—have, while their
lives may have but faintly answered to the
touch, witnessed the same confession.

One more passage, and I have done with this
unworthy attempt to say a little about a profoundly influential life.   It is part of the noble
ending to the pregnant and powerfully written
essay on 'The Incarnation and Principles of
Evidence.' It may be said, no doubt, that the
passage about to be quoted was written long
ago, and that views change with years.   The
words are, however, taken from the fourth
edition, revised, of the 'Theological Essays,'
published as late as 1895. When the second
edition of the work appeared, its author wrote
an elaborate preface dealing with what he called
the change in the temper of English thought.

The third edition came without additional preface, and the fourth likewise, and I for one cannot but believe that, in allowing the words to remain in his revised fourth edition, a man of so extreme a conscientiousness as was Mr Hutton (who, let it be remembered, withdrew an essay on George Eliot from one of his books, because he perceived she had still to publish works which might prove his criticism unjust) intended that these words should stand as his mature and inspiring confession of faith. The words are these :—

'And now, to come to an end, let me ask myself and answer the question as truly as I can, whether this great, this stupendous, fact of the Incarnation is honestly *believable* by any ordinary man of modern times, who has not been educated into it, but educated to distrust it, who has no leaning to the *orthodox* creed as such, but has very generally preferred to associate with heretics, who is quite alive to the force of the scientific and literary scepticisms of his day, who has no antiquarian tastes, no predilection for the venerable past, who does not regard this truth as part of a great system, dogmatic or ecclesiastical, but merely for itself, who is, in a word, simply anxious to take hold, if so he may, of any divine hand stretched out to help him through the excitements and the languor, the joy, the sorrow, the storm and sunshine, of this unintelligible life? From my heart I answer Yes—believable, and more than believable in any mood in which we can rise above ourselves to that super-natural spirit which orders the "unruly wills and affections of sinful men," *more* than believable, I say, because it so vivifies and supplements that fundamental faith in God as to realise what were otherwise abstract, and without dissolving the mystery, to clothe eternal love with breathing life.'

These are not lightly written words : they are words of weighty and solemn import. Well for him who has hidden under the verbal expression of his creed, be that what it may, as ardent a search after truth, as rich a burden of humility, as noble a record of honourable life ! 'Almost a great man,' said the *Saturday Review*. Mr Frederick Greenwood's words are better worth remembering :— 'He was all conscience that was not thought ; justice his constant aim, and humanity his strongest inspiration.' This witness is true. He drew from men by the silent force of his character, a kind of sanction to their being rebuked by him, which in some measure upheld him in his opposition to many of their own weaknesses. He was deaf to the call of mere fashion or faction ; impervious to the attraction of a bought - with - a - price popularity ; resolute in what he conceived to be his duty. To know him was to be able to predict the path he would take. Surely these lines, written

H

of another, are even more appropriate to
Richard Holt Hutton :—

> ' But he preserved from chance control
> The fortress of his 'stablisht soul ;
> In all things sought to see the whole ;
> Brooked no disguise ;
> And set his heart upon the goal,
> Not on the prize.'

THE END

www.ingramcontent.com/pod-product-compliance
Lightning Source LLC
Chambersburg PA
CBHW032144010726
47493CB00008BA/2574